MW01707710

After the Broken Heart:

Finding the Love of Christ

May God bring
healing to all
your wounds.
May His love
fill you to
complete.
Eda

After the Broken Heart: Finding the Love of Christ

Eda Maddalena

New Author Publishing
Brockville, Ontario Canada

After the Broken Heart:
Finding the Love of Christ

ISBN 978-1-928045-10-6

Cover photograph taken by Adam Maddalena featuring Aaron Maddalena on the Island of Capri.(From darkness to the light of Christ)

New Author Publishing
Brockville, Ontario Canada
www.newauthorpublishing.com

Dedication:

This book was inspired by the Holy Spirit, and I give all the praise and glory to God.

Thank you to Jesus for loving me. To my two beautiful sons, Adam and Aaron, who are my two most precious gifts given to me by the Lord. They have shown me great love, courage, and support. I love you both with all my heart. I also want to thank my mother for leading me to Christ. I am grateful to all who prayed for me and were an example of God's love and grace. Thank you to Peter and Sharon for teaching me to always have hope. To Judi for her beautiful, spirit-filled counseling sessions and prayers. To my family and friends who supported me. I love you all.

Contents

After the Broken Heart

He heals the brokenhearted and binds up their wounds [curing their pains and their sorrows].

Psalm 147: 3 AMP

Where is the Love?

There are no scars or bruises on the outside for people to see.
But look deep inside the broken heart of a woman.
Deep within are the scars and bruises of lies, rejection, and abandonment.
Deep within are the cries of a woman.

Where is the love?

Deep inside her heart is the desire to love and be loved.
To be loved by her husband as Christ loved the church.
He gave Himself up for her.
To be lovely and beautiful are the deep longings of a woman's heart.

Take care of me.
Help me feel safe.
Tell me you love me as I am.
Tell me you see my beauty.
Spend time with me.
Look deep into my eyes.
Speak to me.
Honour me as your wife.

I cannot honour you, he said.
I feel no connection to you.
I feel empty inside.
We have nothing in common.

Oh Lord, Where is the love?

Help me Lord, I cried.
The family I once knew is gone.
I feel so ashamed.
I feel so confused.
Where can I run?
Where can I hide?
When will this hurt and shame subside?

Divorce is ok, I was told.
My mind cannot understand how this could be.
Where is the love in the breaking of a promise?
Where is the love in the breaking of a covenant?
We promised to love each other in good times and in bad.
Until death do us part.

Where is the love my dearest Saviour?

It is going to get dark, I heard him say.
Lord, help me break free from this darkness that surrounds me.
My mind and emotions are being manipulated.
What evil has caused a man to be burdened with guilt and shame?
He no longer sees me.
He cannot look into my eyes.
Dear Jesus, there is only emptiness inside.

You will find someone else.
I must go.
I am out the door.
I am not happy here.

Why? Why?
He left me my Father.
He abandoned me.
Save me Lord!
Have mercy on me!
I cried out from the depths of my soul.
Jesus, I am pleading with you desperately.
I cannot bear this pain.
I am all alone.
What shall I do?
I cannot sleep here alone in my bed.
My mind is in deep darkness and silence.

Where, oh, where is the love?

My heart is broken for my children.
They no longer have the family they once knew.
The future I dreamed of has vanished.
Where is the love?
I cannot see it through the lies of a man.
All I see is broken promises.
Help me find You, Lord, in this deep pit of despair

My self-worth as a woman is gone.
I want to hide beneath my bed, never to come out again.
What if I were prettier, taller, smarter, thinner?
Would he have stayed?
Would he have loved me then?
Would he have treated me with dignity and worth?

I asked again and again for the truth.
Why are you unhappy?
Why did you leave me?
But my questions went unanswered.
How can I find the truth Lord?
Why did he leave me all alone?

Oh God, the lies torment my mind?
The nights seem so long, with no answers.
Twisted words keep me in darkness.
My heart longs for truth.
My mind cannot find rest.
The lies confuse and suffocate me.

Where is the Love?

The Lord gently guides me to see the truth with my own eyes.
Knowing deep inside that he would be there.
My heart pounds with pain to reach the place of final truth.
Someone else has taken my place.
I cannot find my breath.
How can this be?
Who is this man, but a stranger to me?
Liar! Cheater! I screamed.
Oh the pain! Oh the grief!
God Help Me, Please!

Where is the Love?

Why didn't he tell me the truth from the beginning Lord?
How could someone you love and trust deceive you for so long?
Help me Lord, I don't understand.
How will I ever trust again?

The marriage was not perfect; far from it my Lord.
I made mistakes and carried pain from my past.
But unconditional love, honesty, and truth are what you desire.
Love one another as I have loved you is your command.

Where is the love?

You told me Lord, that you collect all my tears in a bottle in heaven.
Your mercy and love have slowly healed and mended my broken heart.
You filled me with courage and strength to face the truth of my marriage.
A truth I could not bear on my own.
You gave Your Son's blood that has washed me clean.
You told me that You have taken me out of the bondage of infidelity.

With a grateful heart Lord,
I thank You that Your truth has set me free.
For You alone are my Redeemer.

Through the lies and abandonment of a man,
I have found the glory of God.
I have found the healing power of Christ's love.
I have found a faith renewed.
I have found a strength I never knew.
I have found the strength of Jesus.
For when I am weak, He is strong.
I have found joy.
I have found God's love for me.
A love I never knew.
His love has shown me that I am a loving and beautiful woman.
I am worthy to be loved.
I am worthy to be treated with dignity and respect.

You are not a victim, I heard the Lord say.
You have victory in Me.
Now pick up the pieces and rebuild your home.
This time build it on My solid foundation.
This foundation is made of truth, love, faith, and knowledge.
The base of this foundation is My power, and it will last into eternity.

Know the power that dwells within you, the Lord said.
I have sent the Holy Spirit to guide you.
My resurrection power is steadfast.
I will never leave you nor forsake you.
I am the Rock.
Place your trust in Me.

Forgive this man, the Lord said.
Let go of your anger and give your burdens to Me.
This is all so difficult Lord.
I know that obedience is necessary to be free.
I choose to forgive him as You have forgiven me.

Please, dear God, take him into Your hands.
Bring healing to his brokenness.
Cleanse him with Your precious blood.
Bless him.
Help him find the power of Your love and forgiveness.

I know that God is the teacher and the judge.
He is the vindicator of all things.
It is time to rebuild my life on His solid ground.
It is time to give all that I am to Jesus.
It is time to do His will here on Earth.
It is time to understand that I am loved by My Heavenly Father.

I am the apple of His eye.

I choose to love and forgive.
I desire to be more like Jesus.
I want to live a life full of joy, love, and peace.
Strengthen my faith each day Lord.
I will trust You.
I will turn to You in times of trouble.

Lord, let Your love transform me and radiate through me.
Use me to touch the lives of your lost sheep.

"Where is the Love?" I once asked.

I found it in *Jesus Christ*.
His Love is Perfect.
Perfect love casts out all fear.
We must live in love, if we are to live in God.
To live in God is to love others—Perfectly!

IT IS TIME TO SHARE THE GOOD NEWS OF JESUS' PERFECT LOVE.
AND SO MY JOURNEY BEGINS.

From Despair to Gladness

The pain of abandonment is difficult to bear
It can lead one to complete despair

What you once knew is gone forever
The choice of someone to love you never

Unanswered questions swimming in your head
Grief and loneliness lie with you in bed

So many things were left unsaid
The emptiness inside feels lonely and dead

The future is unclear and love is gone
A heart in small pieces, everything wrong

A mind that searches for peace at last
Will never find it in the past

A search that has led to a healing
Was found at first not to be appealing

A new heart and mind must be desired
If darkness and lies are to be retired

Darkness is scattered by God's own Word
Lies exposed no longer heard

To find the greatest love of all
The love of Christ who carries us when we fall

For He too knows our human pain
He came down from Heaven to be slain

He shed His blood to set us free
The future with Christ is very clear to see

A future filled with peace, joy, and love
Beautiful gifts from Heaven above

To follow Christ we need to decide
Do not run from this truth and hide

The light of Christ is deep within
Do not let this light grow dim

Ignite the fire, let the flame burn
The passion of Christ, we need to learn

His love forever etched in our heart
We were created not to be apart

For the one who created you called you into being
Turn to Him, repent instead of fleeing

The worldly things will leave you thirsting for more
For our sins, our pain, and our sorrows He bore

Come out of your despair and sadness
Rejoice, Rejoice with Him in gladness

Finding the Love of Christ

For God so loved the world that he gave his one and only Son, that whoever believes in him shall not perish but have eternal life.

John 3:16

My Forever Girl

You are My forever girl
Forever loved
Forever beside Me
Forever blessed
Forever Mine
My forever girl
Forever beautiful
Forever in Me
Forever united to Me
Always and Forever loved
The beauty of you will be
Forever etched in My Heart

For great is his love toward us, and the faithfulness of the Lord endures forever

Psalm 117:2

We Are One

My heart belongs to you
Will you reach out and take a piece
And bring it close to yours
Together We are one
One in love
One in peace
One in joy

But the person united with the Lord becomes one spirit with Him.

1 Corinthians 6:17 AMP

Love Pours Down

My love pours down on you
Like rain from a cloud
As rain nourishes the flowers
So My love nourishes your soul
Soak in My love
Let it feed every cell of your being
Let My love fill you to overflowing
Let My love pour out of you
As water from a spout
Nourishing everyone around you

And hope does not put us to shame, because God's love has been poured into our heart through the Holy Spirit, who has been given to us.

Romans 5:5

Believe

Dream big
Desire Me
Put Me first
See how I make things new
See the transforming power of My love
Place your hope in Me
Trust in Me
Love Me
Find joy in Me
Delight in My presence
I will give you the desires of your heart
Believe in Me

Believe in the Lord Jesus, and you will be saved --- you and your household.

Acts 16:31

Great Delight

My heart cannot contain the love I feel for you
It bursts with excitement every time you spend time with Me
I treasure your time spent in prayer
You bring a smile to My face
I am so proud of you
Your beauty is so radiant
I take great delight in you
Listening to you
You honour Me when you give Me the gift of time
I find great pleasure in hearing your voice speak words of love to Me
I love to be near to you as you draw near to Me.

Draw close to God and He will draw close to you.

James 4:8 AMP

A Longing

I love you
I long to see you rejoice
I long to see you thankful
I long to see you worship
I long to see you pray
I long to see you at rest in Me
I long to see you love Me

Be happy [in your faith] and rejoice and be glad-hearted continually (always);

1 Thessalonians 5:16 AMP

Healing The Broken Heart

Let Me tear down that wall
You built around your heart
Let My love bind every wound
Let My love heal your broken heart
Let My love bring you out of the pit of despair
Let My love open your heart
Receive all that I have for you
For I have much
And I will shower you with My goodness
Will you receive it?

He lifted me out of the slimy pit, out of the mud and mire; he set my feet on a rock.

Psalm 40:2

Perfect Love

In My arms there is no fear
There is perfect love
In My arms there is no rejection
There is acceptance
In My arms there is no abandonment
There is unity
In My arms there are no lies
There is truth
In My arms there is no loneliness
There is friendship
In My arms you will find rest
You will find perfect, perfect peace

You will keep in perfect peace those whose minds are steadfast, because they trust in you.

Isaiah 26:3

The Greatest Gift

Oh how beautiful is your soul
When it is resting in Me
When it is trusting in Me
My glory light is able to shine
Brightly through this soul
I can use you to bring forth that glory to others
At rest you will show others
My gift of faith
My gift of hope
My greatest gift of all
LOVE

And now these three remain; faith, hope and love, But the greatest of these is love.

1Corinthians 13:13

Unconditional Love

In My love there is truth
The truth that I gave My only Son
To show you the depth, height, and length of My love
In the shed blood there is love
In the sacrifice there is love
In the offering there is love
In the cross there is love
Look deep into the eyes of My Son, Jesus
You will see perfect love
Unconditional love
A faithful love that endures forever

For the Lord is good and his love endures forever

Psalm 100:5

Shining Star

You are My shining star
Shine brightly My love
Let My love flow freely
Into you as it overflows
Freely out of you
Love others as I love you
Have no fear
Love completely
As I love you, completely

Then you will shine among them like stars in the sky.

Philippians 2:15

The Lamb

I am the Lamb that was slain
My blood is offered for you
My sacrifice is a gift to you
A gift of My deep red
Passionate love for you
Bathe in My love
Soak in it
Cleanse yourself in it
My love will bring
Freedom from all your bondages
It is My free will offering to you
So that you may have life
And have it more abundantly

"I am the good shepherd. The good shepherd lays down His life for the sheep."

John 10:11

My Love is Sufficient

Be filled with My love
Let My love light shine
In every area of your life
Be filled, be full
My loving-kindness is sufficient for you

"My grace is sufficient for you, for my power is made perfect in your weakness."

2 Corinthians 12:9

The Cross

The cross is My love for you

My love is Tender

My love Transforms

My love Teaches

My love Takes you higher

My love Totally gives

My love Totally forgives

My love Totally heals

My love wipes away all Transgressions

My love resTores

My love is perfecT

YOU ARE COMPLETE IN ME

And in Christ you have been brought to fullness.

Colossians 2:10

Truth

My love is a blanket
It covers you and brings warmth
It warms the entire body
Let My love bring warmth
To your mind
Understand how deep is My love
Let My love bring warmth
To your heart
Feel my never ending love
Let my love bring warmth
To your soul
We will be one in spirit
One in truth
One in perfect union

O Send me Your light and Your truth, let them lead me.

Psalm 43:3 AMP

Free Indeed

Let My love set you free from the prison of your sin
My love is the key that will open the door to freedom
Open your heart to receive My love
Look into My eyes on the cross
See My suffering
See My pain
See My love
A gift to you to set you on the path of freedom and truth
Take the path less travelled
And you will be free indeed
For whom the Son sets free is free indeed

So if the Son sets you free, you will be free indeed.

John 8:36

No Fear

In My love is glorious light
There can be no darkness
Step into My love light
Let My glory surround you
My love will give you strength
You will face every trial with courage
My love casts out all fear
There is no fear in perfect love
My love gives you power
My love gives you a sound mind
My love is perfect

There is no fear in love. But perfect love drives out fear

1John 4:18

Jesus is Love

O Glorious Love
O Righteous Love
O Wonderful Love
O Mighty Love
O Beautiful Love
O Compassionate Love
O Unconditional Love
O Peaceful Love
O Joyous Love
O Unending Love
O Healing Love
O Forgiving Love
O Sacrificial Love
O Unbinding Love
O All Encompassing Love
O Love, Thy true name is JESUS

Greater love has no one than this: to lay down one's life for a friend.

John 15:13

An Everlasting Love

Let go of pretense
Let go of worldly ways
Let go of sin
Let go of being right
Let go of trying to control
Let go of striving
Do you not know that you do not earn My love
I have loved you with an everlasting love
I have called you and you are Mine
I have given My Son freely
Your debts are paid in full
Accept My love as a free will offering to you
With Love from Me to you
You will be everything I created you to be

Do not fear, for I have redeemed you; I have summoned you by name; you are mine.

Isaiah 43:1

Desires of Your Heart

I know the desires of your heart
Trust in My love
Let Me do a work in you
Let Me transform you
Let Me heal you
Let Me melt away all your pain
Let Me carry your heavy burdens
Allow Me to come deep into your heart
Allow Me to hold your heart in the palm of My hand
And breathe love and life into the brokenness
My love will make you whole

Take delight in the Lord and he will give you the desires of your heart.

Psalm 37:4

Draw Near

Draw near to Me
I will draw near to you
Pull up a chair
Sit at the foot of My cross
My blood is love
A sacrificial love
A love that covers all sin
A love that cleanses
Find joy at the cross
Find peace at the cross
Bathe in My love
Soak in My love
Be covered in a love freely given

You will be like a well-watered garden, like a spring whose waters never fail.

Isaiah 58:11

Seek, Knock, Ask

My dearest child
My love will never forsake you
I will not leave you orphaned
Reach out to Me
Receive My love
I will never hurt you
I will forgive you as far
As the east is from the west
I will honour you as My child
In Me you will find wholeness
You will be complete
In Me you will be My chosen one
My love is true
My love is pure
My love is clean

My love is for you and with you
My love is in you
Seek and you will find
Knock and the door will be opened
Ask and you shall receive
My love freely given,
Freely poured out
From My heart to yours

As far as the east is from the west, so has He removed our transgressions from us.

Psalm 103:12 AMP

Old Rags

Stand tall beside Me
Take My hand
Let Me lead you
Allow Me to guide you
No one can give you love that equals Mine
Take off the old rags
Put on My love
You will find your true self
You will find the you I created you to be
You will be at peace with yourself
You will be able to love as I have commanded you to love

I give you a new commandment: that you should love one another. Just as I have loved you, so you too should love one another.

John 13:34 AMP

Love Light

My love is a light that can never be extinguished
It glows inside you
Ready to share into the world
Will you let go of the pain
It dims My light in you
Let Me carry your pain and burdens
Let My love be enough for you
Nothing can compare to My Love
Nothing can fill your emptiness
Take time to rest in Me
See how My love fills You
You will be satisfied

Come to me, all you who are burdened and I will give you rest.

Matthew 11:28

Fragrant Offering

You are like a beautiful flower
In My bouquet
Lovely and alive
Each one of you is a unique flower
The more you allow My love to flow
The more fragrant you become
Let My fragrance fill the Earth

And walk in the way of love, just as Christ loved us and gave himself up for us a fragrant offering and sacrifice to God.

Ephesians 5:2

Fire

Allow Me into your heart
Let My love set you on fire
A fire that burns deep within
A fire that will never be extinguished
It is fueled by an everlasting love
My love
My love
My love for you

He will baptize you with the Holy Spirit and with fire.

Luke 3:16 AMP

Fruit

Come to My cross and place your gifts before Me
Your pain
Your sorrows
Your past
Your present
Your future
Your family
Your finances
Your strengths
Your weakness
Everything entrusted to Me
My gifts to you in return
My Unending Love

Joy
Peace
Patience
Kindness
Self-Control
Hope
Courage
Healing
Wisdom
Grace
Mercy
Redemption
Forgiveness
Truth
Each gift I give is stamped with My Love

Peace I leave with you my peace I give you.

John 14:27

Heals All Wounds

My love dissipates pain
My love sets the captives free
My love heals all wounds
My love brings salvation
My love breaks the chains that bind
My love reveals truth
My love opens blind eyes
My love is unconditional
My love is sacrificially given
It is given to heal the broken hearted
It is given to bind up every wound

He has sent me to proclaim freedom for the prisoners.

Luke 4:18

No Beginning and No End

My love for you is endless
It has no beginning
It has no end
It is forever and forever
And forever more
Soak in it
Understand the depths of it
I knew you before I formed you in the womb
My love overflows and is abundant
Drink it in
Absorb it into every cell of your being
Allow it to overflow to others
Give to others
This love I give to you
Be merciful
Love tenderly
You are My precious bride

I am the Alpha and the Omega, the First and the Last, the Beginning and the End.

Revelation 22:13

Everlasting Light

My Love
You are radiant in My light
You shine out among the darkness
You make everything new
Your light has no beginning and no end
Follow Me
You will have everlasting light

The sun shall no more be your light by day, nor for brightness shall the moon give light to you, but the Lord shall be to you an everlasting light.

Isaiah 60: 19

Everlasting Love

Give to Me all your burdens
I will give you peace
Give to Me all your sorrows
I will give you joy
Give to Me all your anger
I will give you forgiveness
Give to Me all your hatred
I will give you love
A love beyond comprehension
Beyond understanding
Beyond reasoning
A love Everlasting

And to know this love that surpasses knowledge—that you may be filled to the measure of all the fullness of God.

Ephesians 3:19

My Dove

My rose, My dove
Do not question My Love
Receive it
Embrace it
Digest it
Let the light of My Love
Shine from you
Shine
Shine
Shine

Oh, how beautiful! Your eyes behind your veil are doves.

Song of Songs 4:1

Be My Hands and Feet

My hope is in you
My joy is in you
My peace is in you
My love is in you
Take off the old rags
Put on the New
Be a new creation
Be My hands
Be My feet
Show the world My great love for them

Therefore, if anyone is in Christ, the new creation has come: The old has gone, the new is here!

2 Corinthians 5:17

Outstretched Arms

Love is My gift to you
Wrapped in My blood
Wrapped in My scars
Wrapped in My dying
Wrapped in My rising
Wrapped in My outstretched arms
Take My hand
Look deep into My eyes
See the love outpoured

In Him we have redemption through his blood, the forgiveness of sins.

Ephesians 1:7

A Clean Heart

Come close to Me
Do not be afraid
Do not be ashamed
I will create in you
A clean heart
Come to Me
Step closer
Look deeply
I pour out My Love
Drink it in
My Love will transform

Create in me a clean heart, O God, and renew a right, persevering, and steadfast spirit within me.

Psalm 51: 10 AMP

Live in Me

Live in Me
I will live in you
In Me you will find
Truth and Freedom
Faith and Hope
Peace and Justice
Love and Forgiveness
Grace and Mercy
Redemption and Salvation
Restoration and Reconciliation
Understanding and Knowledge
An overwhelming
Abundant Joy

But let all who take refuge in you be glad; let them ever sing for joy.

Psalm 5:11

Trust in Love

My love is wide
My love is deep
My love encompasses everything
Give yourself to Me
Trust in My love for you
Hear My Love Songs
Lean your ear to Me
As I whisper
My Darling, I love you

Trust in the Lord with all your heart and lean not on your own understanding.

Proverbs 3:5

Always With You

Hold Me tight
Never let Me go
Don't you see Me
I am always with you
My Love endures forever
And a day

Give thanks to the Lord, for he is good; his love endures forever!

Psalm 118:1

The Shepherd

Sing Glory to My Name
As I sing your name
As I sing a love song
Into your heart
As I sing
I love you forever songs
Hear My voice
As sheep know the Shepherd's voice
Follow My song of love
That leads you close to My heart
A heart that will hold you forever

My sheep listen to my voice; I know them, they follow me.

John 10:27

I Am Love

Great is My Love
I AM Love
I embody Love
Love is My Name
Love is in Me
Love surrounds Me
Love is poured out to you
Be filled
You will fill others
Give and it will be given to you

Whoever does not love does not know God, because God is love.

1John 4:8

The Risen Lord

See Me the Risen Lord
Look upon My beautiful face
See the Glory
See the Mercy
See the Grace
See the Scars
See the LOVE

He is not here; He is risen, as He said [He would do]. Come, see the place where he lay.

Matthew 28:6 AMP

Release Your Burdens

Let My Love be enough
Give up doing and striving
Give up controlling
Release your burdens to Me
Open your arms
My love is being outpoured
To fill you completely
Open wide your arms
Tear down the walls that protect
The false walls
Open your heart to Me
Let My Love comfort you
Let My Love surround you
Let My Love bring healing
Healing you long for in your heart
Receive

We love Him, because he first loved us.

1John 4:19 AMP

I Am Here

Do you not see Me
I am here
Right beside you
Holding your hand
Look down
See your face tattooed
On the palm of My hand
With a heart that says
"The Love of My Life"

Behold, I have indelibly imprinted (tattooed a picture of) you on the palm of each of My hands.

Isaiah 49:16 AMP

The Bride

Come dance with Me
The dance of Love
The dance of a bride and groom
Look into My eyes
See My heart
It beats for you
Feel the beat of My heart
Next to yours
Our hearts beat as one

You have stolen my heart, my sister, my bride; you have stolen my heart.

Song of Songs 4:9

Chosen One

Gracious and Merciful
Loving and Forgiving
Ready to receive you as you are
Come
Come closer
Lean your ear to Me
Hear Me whisper your name
You are My most precious
Chosen one

But you are a chosen people, a royal priesthood, a holy nation, God's special possession.

1 Peter 2:9

All of Me

A heart that completely trusts Me
Takes My breath away
A mind open to My truth
Delights Me
A soul drawn to Me
I will wrap My arms around
To comfort and console you
And give you All of ME

But blessed is the one who trusts in the Lord, whose confidence is in him.

Jeremiah 17:7

My Handiwork

You are My creation
My masterpiece
You are My perfect handiwork
My workmanship
Created to Love Me
To worship Me
To give yourself freely
To do My will
Do not fear My Love
It has the power to transform you

For we are God's handiwork, created in Christ Jesus for good works which God prepared in advance for us to do.

Ephesians 2:10

At the Cross

Stand in the presence of My Love
Are you at the cross?
Do you see My Love?
Each drop of blood is filled with love
Do not hide
Do not run away
Run TO My cross
The gift you long for is there
The gift that will complete you
It will make you whole
The gift that never runs dry
The gift that will
Quench every desire
Every need
Every longing fulfilled
Here at the cross

But [you were purchased] with the precious blood of Christ (the Messiah), like that of a [sacrificial]; lamb without blemish or spot.

1 Peter 1: 19 AMP

Good Gifts

My heart aches for you
Oh how I long to Love you
To lavish unto you
All that I have to give
To give you the desires of your heart
Oh how I long to give My children
Good gifts
Be thankful and savour each gift
Given from Me
To you
Your Father
God

If you then, though you are evil, know how to give good gifts to your children, how much more will your Father in heaven give the Holy Spirit to those who ask him!

Luke 11:13

Eyes on Me

New Hope
New desires
New joys
New ways of doing things
Will come to you
Keep your eyes on Me
Keep your focus on Me

Fixing our eyes on Jesus, the pioneer and perfecter of faith.

Hebrews 12:2

River of Blood

There is a river of blood
The blood that flows from My heart
To yours
Filling you with My life
A life devoted to ME
For in Me you can do all things
In Me you can find the love
You are thirsting for
In Me you are complete

I have strength for all things in Christ Who empowers me

Philippians 4:13   AMP

Be Still

My eyes see only you
I walk beside you
At all times
My heart beats with yours
Be still
You will hear it
Beating the greatest words spoken
I Love You
See I have given My Son for you
I Love You

Be still and know that I am God.

Psalm 46:10

The Alpha and The Omega

I am the Alpha and the Omega
The beginning and the end
My words bring life
My words will endure
Look in My words
You will see My passion
For all of creation
You love
Because I first loved you
I created you
I formed you in the womb
I know every hair on your head
Look deep into My heart
There you are
Safe and sound

"I am the Alpha and the Omega," says the Lord God, "who is and who was, and who is to come, the Almighty".

Revelation 1:8

Pick Up Your Cross

My children
Hear My voice
Pick up your cross
Follow the trail of My blood
It will lead you to the greatest
Love story ever told

Then Jesus said to his disciples, "Whoever wants to be my disciple must deny themselves and take up their cross and follow me"

Matthew 16:24

Grace-Filled Love

Your heart
Your heart
Forever beating
In My hands
As I love you
As I cover you
As I transform you
With a tender and compassionate
Grace-filled love

Let us then approach God's throne of grace with confidence, so that we may receive mercy and find grace to help us in our time of need

Hebrews 4:16

I Send You

As the Father has sent Me
So I send you
Love with an open heart
Give without wanting in return
Receive with a grateful heart

As the Father has sent me, so I am sending you.

John 20:21

Nothing Can Compare

Love never fails
Nothing can compare
To the Love I have for you
You are My everything
You are My princess bride
You are My daughter
Standing in My light
Let your light shine
For all to see
Be My light

And I will be a Father to you, and you shall be My sons and daughters, says the Lord Almighty.

2 Corinthians 6:18 AMP

Covered In The Blood

All your brokenness
All your darkness
All your hurts
All your worries
All your anxieties
All of it
Nailed to the cross
Covered in My blood
Signed
I LOVE YOU
JESUS

He has taken it away, nailing it to the cross.

Colossians 2:14

Greatest Love Story

The Greatest Love Story
Is My Love for you
Perfect
Everlasting
Never Ending
No beginning and no end
Forever and Ever
Amen

From everlasting to everlasting the Lord's love is with those who fear him.

Psalm 103:17

Abounding Love

Abounding in love
Is My heart for you
Surrounded by My Love are you
Astounded by the Miracles
I will do for you
When you rest in My Love
And trust in My Love
See the small miracles
Observe the great miracles
My love can produce
Love Me as I love you

The Lord is compassionate and gracious; slow to anger, abounding in love.

Psalm 103:8

Power and Strength

Rest beside Me
My arms are opened wide
I have strength
I have power
I have love
Come to Me
I will give you
These gifts
Rest in Me

For it is in Him that all things were created, in heaven and on earth, things seen and things unseen.

Colossians 1:16 AMP

Close to Me

Walk beside Me
Hand in hand
As I bring your hand to My lips
A kiss of love
A love that flows
From My heart to yours
You are My first love
And My last love
I hold you close to Me
I will always love you
Forever

Blessed are those you choose and bring near to live in your courts!

Psalm 65:4

Every Wound

Remain in Me
And I will remain in you
Love as I love you
Give as I give to you
Humble yourself before Me
Allow Me into
The deepest places of your heart
Let Me go deeper
Into the depths of your pain
Let My love heal every wound

Remain in me, as I also remain in you.

John 15:4

Conquered

Look on the cross
Look in the tomb
They are empty
I have risen
I have conquered
Sin and Death
My resurrection power
Dwells within you
Don't cover up this power
Let it flow freely
Know My healing power
It is real
It comes from My love for you

But thanks be to God! He gives us victory through our Lord Jesus Christ.

1 Corinthians 15:57

Yesterday, Today, and Forever

Come to Me
Do not be afraid
Come as you are
My love washes away
All that has stained you
My love makes you new again
I am faithful
I am trustworthy
I am always with you
I am God
The same Yesterday
Today
Forever

Jesus Christ is the same, yesterday and today and forever.

Hebrews 13:8

Agape

I take such joy in loving you
My pride and joy
Are you
My child
My love for you
Can never be measured
It is never ending
Overflowing
In abundance
It is Agape

Love does not delight in evil but rejoices in the truth.

1 Corinthians 13:6

Beautiful

My little darling daughter
How precious to Me
You were created in My image
Your beauty outshines the stars
You are radiant in My sight
I dwell inside you
Hear My voice
Hear My love songs
How beautiful
How beautiful
How beautiful
You are to Me

So God created mankind in his own image.

Genesis 1:27

Be Bold

Trust in Me
Rest in Me
Hold onto Me
Rely on Me
Speak to Me
Come to Me
Find strength in Me
Be bold
Be filled with the knowledge
Of My love for you

Therefore, since we have such a hope, we are very bold.

2 Corinthians 3:12

Healing Minds

Glorious love
Pouring forth
Flowing freely
Touching lives
Changing hearts
Healing minds
Transforming My children
Into My Image

For the Spirit God gave us does not make us timid, but gives us power, love and self-discipline.

2 Timothy 1:7

The Way, The Truth, The Life

Every drop of blood
Is filled with love
I see every tear you shed
My deep wounds
Bore your pains
Pick up your cross
Follow Me
The path is narrow
The burdens are light
My love light
Shines for you to see
The way to Me

I am the way
I am the truth
I am the life
There is no other way
Follow Me
Love Me
See the plans I have for you
I love you deeply

Jesus answered, "I am the way and the truth and the life. No one comes to the Father except through me."

John 14:6.

The Great I AM

My bride
Spotless and blameless
Turn your hearts to Me
Give yourselves freely
Completely
Trust in My love
Trust in My providence
Trust in My timing
I will never disappoint
I will never abandon
I will always love
Love is who I am
The Great I AM

And God said to Moses, I AM WHO I AM and WHAT I AM, and I WILL BE WHAT I AM;

Exodus 3:14 AMP

All Things New

A childhood lost
Will be renewed
I make all things new
My love transforms
My love renews
All may seem lost
Look to Me
You will find
Everything you have ever longed for

And He Who is seated on the throne said, See! I make all things new.

Revelation 21:5 AMP

Abba Father

Call Me Father
Abba Father
Your Daddy
I will protect you
I will guide your footsteps
I will hold your hand
I will pick you up when you fall
I will kiss your wounds
I will lift you up
Up to the heart of a
Loving Father
Abba Father

And because you are his sons, God sent the Spirit of His Son into our hearts, the spirit who cries out, "Abba Father!"

Galatians 4:6

A Sacrifice

I came
I came to love you
I came in the flesh
I came as a sacrifice
I came as the Lamb
The Lamb that was slain
I am inside you
My love dwells deep within you

The word became flesh and made his dwelling among us.

John 1:14

Dance With Joy

Let your hearts dance
Dance with joy
Joy in knowing
That you are deeply loved
Deeply, deeply loved
I send My angels
To sing to you
My glorious love songs
Can you hear them
Singing
You are My most precious
My most beautiful
My greatest creation
I formed you in
Your mother's womb
Sealed with love

You have turned my wailing into dancing; you have removed my sackcloth and clothed me with joy.

Psalm 30:11

Grateful Heart

O how a grateful heart
Brings Me such great joy
To see My Children
Full of Thanksgiving
Brings Me great delight
I delight in you
Please delight in Me
See the beauty in all
I do for you
See My loving hand
Covering and protecting
My dearest, dearest
Child
Hold My hand
Let Me
Direct your steps

Give thanks in all circumstances

1 Thessalonians 5:18

Seasons

There are seasons
My child
Know that My Love
Is with you
In every season of your life
My love will never
Be overshadowed
By your difficulties
My love shines
Even more brightly
In those seasons
It may seem cold
But look to Me
And receive
The warmth and
Protection
Of My Love

To everything there is a season, and a time for every matter or purpose under heaven.

Ecclesiastes 3:1 AMP

Childlike Faith

It is all about love
Love heals
Love sacrifices
Love is selfless
Love is endless
Love covers and protects
I am LOVE
Have childlike faith
You will know Love
Even more deeply
Than you can ever
Imagine
Believe

Therefore, whoever takes the lowly position of this child is the greatest in the kingdom of heaven.

Matthew 18:4

Your Heart

When I close My eyes
I see your face
I will never forget you
You are perfect
As I see your heart
I pour out My love
Filling it
Let Me fill it to overflow

For the Lord sees not as man sees; for man looks on the outward appearance, but the Lord looks on the heart.

1 Samuel 16:7 AMP

Thirsting

My heart longs for you
My heart beats for you
My desire is to be near you
Close to you
Close enough
To hear your heartbeat
Beating for Me
Desiring My Love
Wanting to be near to Me
Thirsting for Me
Hungry for Me
Know how deeply
I love you

But whoever takes a drink of the water that I give him shall never, no never be thirsty any more.

John 4:14 AMP

A Narrow Path

Trust
Joy
Gratitude
Prayer
Love
Service
Forgiveness
A narrow path to walk
Let My will be done

But small is the gate and narrow the road that leads to life.

Matthew 7:14

It Is Finished

It is finished
Are the words spoken on the cross
Do you not see
I have taken it all
All your burdens
All your pain
All your sorrow
My faithful love endures forever

He said, It is finished! And bowed His head and gave up His spirit.

John 19:30 AMP

Great Joy

Great Joy
Great Joy
Great Joy is Your Faithfulness
Oh, Lord

Because of the Lord's great love we are not consumed, for his compassions never fail. They are new every morning; great is your faithfulness.

Lamentations 3:22-23

MY PRAYER IS THAT ALL WHO READ THIS WILL BE TOUCHED BY THE HEALING, TRANSFORMING, FORGIVING, AND LOVING POWER OF CHRIST.

A portion of the proceeds of this book with be donated to **Wells of Hope.**

"For Those Who Thirst"
www.wellsofhope.com
1499 Irvine Rd,
Niagara-on-the-Lake, Ontario
Canada
L0S 1J0

40569573R00066

Made in the USA
Charleston, SC
10 April 2015